The Ghost of Every Feathered Thing

PAULA J. LAMBERT

FUTURECYCLE PRESS
www.futurecycle.org

Cover artwork, "Song Sparrow (Melospiza melodia)," copyright © 2020 Kent B. Krugh; cover design by Paula J. Lambert; interior design by Diane Kistner; Palatino text with Playfair and Montserrat titling

Library of Congress Control Number: 2021950109

Published by FutureCycle Press
Athens, Georgia, USA

ISBN 978-1-952593-19-2

for my grandfather
Ralph A. Lambert

Contents

I. In the Beginning

II. The Business of Seeing

III. Knowing What We Need

IV. Off Course

V. What's Holy

I must follow up these continual lessons of the air, water, earth,
I perceive I have no time to lose.

—Walt Whitman

At night, they don't exist, except in our dreams…

—Mary Oliver

I.

In the Beginning

What They Imply by Depicting a Vulture

...because in this race of creatures/there is no male.
—*Hieroglyphics of Horapollo*

In the beginning, all was female. Bird begat bird
begat bird, each impregnated by the wind, which

was also female. In the beginning, vulture was
goddess. For 120 days she was pregnant and for

120 days she cared for her young and for 120 days
she cared for herself, preparing to ride the wind

for the five remaining days of her year. Imagine
being cradled by the breath of the world, levitating

through lovemaking—oh, imagine! In the beginning
we were worshiped, and in the beginning we could fly,

and in the beginning we were loved by the air itself.
In the beginning we created, and in the beginning

Sky bowed to us, and in the beginning Earth reached
for us and, oh, in the beginning we were holy, we were

holy in the beginning, and can you imagine that,
in the beginning, we were holy, we were whole?

HuffPost Science News Headline, or
When You Wish Something More Had Been Lost

The fossilized remains of a primitive Chinese bird,
the article said, show he had feathers on his legs.
Long ones. But HuffPost's headline had promised
more, positing that birds may once have had four
wings, that "extra feathered limbs" might have
helped them to fly. To read these leg-feathers were
only a rudder was a letdown. I'd hoped to discover
birds had evolved from something more delicate
than dinosaurs, that teeth were not all that had been
lost in the process. I wanted to read birds had
descended from seraphim—that angel wings and
birds' wings, flapping furiously, had fused. I wanted
to believe something holy had wanted a closer look
at what God created: trees, berries, beaches, all things
under the sea so hard to discern from so far away.
Angels already know something of wind, but nothing
of clenching: the bark of a sycamore, scales of a fish,
an emerald lawn. I wanted to read the losing of wings
was a wanting and not just a no longer needing.

What It Takes to Be Born

I. Pipping

It begins with a breakthrough—no!

It starts with strangulation, an inability to breathe.
Chick, growing, no longer able to absorb oxygen
through the pores of his shell, expends the muscle
on the back of his neck, lifting the egg tooth
to tear his way through to air. He is not yet free.

That first tender tear through the air sac is time:
a few hours, to wend his way through to hatching.

II. Hatching

The shell is weak: his bones have already absorbed
the calcium they need. Tooth in place, he rotates,
carving a circular line…oh, can opener! Oh, hat!
Oh/breath/oh/air/oh/PUSH/oh/sever/oh/divide!

III. Surrender

What's left is this: a splaying of the body, giving in
to gravity. Rest. Hours more to recognize Hunger,
that driving need for what comes next.

Losing the Egg Tooth

There are two possibilities for what you will feel
when it falls off. First, you think you will die.

You are fierce without it, this tiny tool,
though don't know it yet, and feel yourself defenseless,
trembling through your rising down: prefeathers.

Ah, bird! You might also not notice it at all,
so proud of the beak that's forming, so aware
of the itch at your toes: what might be talons.

My hope for you, fledgling, is that you will suffer,
that loss will form a muscle memory, important later,
when it comes time to wield those claws.

How History Helps Us Survive: Hoatzin

When the nestling spies the viper, letting go
becomes a kind of grace. God is the ghost
of every feathered thing that ever dreamed
of drawing breath. God surrounds us.
And it's not the splash of the river that tells us
we've been saved. It's the sound of what swims
toward us. The new danger. The ongoing need
to survive. History is older than hope.
Newly doused and still missing muscle,
the nestling knows this: how to open his wings.
How to claw his way back to where he belongs.

Chick Ornamentation: American Coot

Feed me, Mother, for
I am beautiful and strong.
I will love you best.

Feed me, Mother, for
I will my own survival.
I shall leave you first.

Feed me, Mother, for
I have no shame, no weakness.
I shall rule these skies.

Feed me, oh Mother!
Oh, nourish and adore me!
Feed me, lest I die.

Feed me, Mother, for
what is dull is meant to die.
Feed me, and watch me rise.

Routine

In March, sea-ice slowly surrounds
Antarctica so ships cannot break

through. Dark, cold, rife with storm,
this is where the emperor penguins

begin their breeding, males offering
an ecstatic display, couples raising

their heads and necks together
in perfect, mirrored form. Each pair

bows, one to the another, holds pose
as if assuaging doubt or guilt, copulates

to produce the single, pale-green,
pear-shaped egg she rolls onto his feet.

For sixty-five days, he incubates
the egg under a fold of skin while she

returns to the sea to feed. He fasts
and tries not to freeze as the fierce

darkness swirls in storms around him
for weeks. Huddled by the hundreds,

backs to the wind, the male emperor
penguins keep each other warm while

they waste away. Their body weight
drops by half before the thick-shelled

eggs beneath them begin to hatch.
It can take three days, just this, chicks

working their way out of the eggs'
thick shells. When they do, the fathers

feed them the curd-like crop-milk
meant to sustain them till their mothers

return. The emperor penguins' breeding
process has taken them through April,

May, June, and now July, when the females
return, if they return—the sea, too, a cruel

mistress. Can you imagine the sound of
each male's call as his mate hauls herself,

fat and fit for the rest of the brooding,
back up onto the ice? It's what she follows

to find him, starving, still reluctant to
leave. Staying in place, even in conditions

like these, has become routine. What
has hatched while waiting, tender and

hungry now, too, opens its mouth for what
its mother has fed on. It takes time for

the males to return comfortably to the sea.
Even then, they come back again and again,

taking turns with their mates, brooding
and foraging, brooding and foraging, until

August turns to September, September to
November, and the chicks molt into full plumage,

finally feeding themselves. It's summer now.
Winter lasted a long, long time. It seems

no wonder, really, that emperor penguins,
faithful as they are to the process, don't mate

for life. Free from the sea-ice, they dive deep
into open waters, surfacing only to breathe.

Gape: Fledglings

every round mouth is a blind wanting
&
the ugly fledgling, naked, needy
gaping

is fed

The Chicken, the Egg

It's a terrible question, really, and one that assumes we don't know the answer. There's no mystery here. Every bird was once a woman, and every woman a man. Every father was once a child, and every child knows to come when she's called. We see the sky reflected in every body of water, need only look down to see up high. Every bird is the same as a star, every star is an egg. When pin feathers blossom and old men die, all of the questions we ask have answers we already know. The answer to every inhale is an exhale. The answer to every breath is to breathe.

The Lunar Landscape of Simple Things

for Kari

It's mindfulness, really, only that,
but to see the surface of something
you hold in your hand—an egg, say,

a set of keys, a single earring—is to
understand what is also vast: this shell,
a lunar surface, whispers *every birth*

begins with the moon. And the carton
this egg comes from says *the forest*
is full of birds, let them wake you.

Each key on the ring has opened a door
that has opened another…or locked it,
tight. And an un-lost earring has endured

loss we think we cannot bear. It's why
we close our fist around it, refusing
to let it go. The lost might be found,

or it might be better off gone. Neither
option negates the beauty of what is
still there. What is the un-lost, really,

but found itself? It's why some keys hang
close to our heart. It's why, sometimes,
we paint the egg, pressing our lips

to a pinhole, blowing softly, whispering
to what might have been a bird: *I need*
you, oh beautiful, beside me forever.

II.

The Business of Seeing

Evolution of the Eyelid: The Business of Seeing

Vestigial in humans, who've learned to cry,
the nictitating membrane—translucent, milky
sometimes—sweeps its horizontal way across

Bird's eye: it's messy business, watching this
world go by. Dangerous, gazing even at what we
love. Ask Eagle, shielding herself from the pointy

beaks of her eager, feeding young, or Woodpecker,
who might otherwise shatter his own retina. Ask
Ostrich, constantly clearing away dry desert sand;

or Goose, goggled, diving for her wet dinner. Bird
stares it all down, never missing what we don't
see, never turning from what makes us blink.

Ubiquity: Sparrow

The sparrow, brown-grey, most familiar of birds,
is unique in this: the extra bone in his tongue.
Sparrow (yard-bird, barn-bird, pest) uses the bone
to stiffen his tongue as he cracks Seed open.

True sparrow, tree sparrow, rock sparrow,
passerine! Fierce in the power of your beak!
Hold tight! hold tight! hold tight!

Oh, to be Sparrow, determined, built for
what he needs. To have in one's mouth not only this
bone, but the muscle which hefts it into place. To be
so firm in our intentions, getting so quickly to Kernel
and spitting out later what we don't need.

The Non-Euclidean Geometry of Human Existence

Crow is capable of traveling that briefer distance,
keeping himself untangled by the brush that binds

our way. We, keen to diversion, wear ourselves out
believing the journey is everything. And so it is:

the grunt, the groan, the lady slipper. Moss, as good
a guide as the sun. The bones of what might have been

Crow peeking through detritus. We've much to learn
and wend our way through all of it, unCrowlike,

seeing with both eyes at once, everything, and cawing.

The Transformative Nature of Disguise: Penguin

Penguin bones are dense, weigh him down, keep him submerged
as his heartbeat slows to something we'd call dead. Penguin,
underwater, has a belly white enough to make him look like ice,

and a back black enough to blend into the surface of the sea.
Penguin is protected for as long as he feels like soaring his salt sky,
unafraid and unaware there are those who think he cannot fly.

Anatomy of Birds, Part 1: Furcula

for Malala Yousafzai

The work of soaring is arduous,
requires more than muscle alone,
requires the delicate architecture
of mostly hollow bone. The fused
and forked clavicle of a bird—
we call it the wishbone—
allows her to bear the rigors of flight,
stretching and then recoiling
with each powerful wingbeat. (Can
you hear it? The fiercely whispered
whoosh, slicing air?) Downstroke
and release. Let's call it resilience,
what pushes the songbird forward,
what propels the hawk! Oh, let's
remember, this living bone can flex!

Anatomy of Birds, Part 2: Common Loon

Flight, for some, is harder work. Take the loon
and his lift-off. We'd like to call it walking on water,
but see it for what it is: a lot of furious flapping

and feet that just get in his way. Blame the bones
that Loon never gains the gift of gliding (not all
the bones of birds are hollow). Blame bad design

for his belly crawl toward the nest. But what keeps
Loon lame on land is what propels the same bird
toward his exquisite submersion, the depths

most dare not plummet. When loons let loose their
lonely cry across the mirrored lake, let yourself cry
back: *Oh, love! I hear you! And I call this My Life!*

The Insistent Nature of Acknowledging Need: Male Swan

for Michael Perkins

It goes on and on, the trachea of a swan, down the S of his throat
and into the complicated coil resting in his sternum. He bellows,

hidden in the reeds, a deep-timbered call powerful enough to both
attract and repel: *Lover, come to me! Foe, stand back!* He need not

work this hard—he is, indeed, all things strong and beautiful. But
it explains the science of the swan song, this tracheal elongation,

his need to acknowledge, in the long, cold note of even a dying
breath, the depth and power of his existence: what it has been,

for him, to cherish and defend. What it has been, for him, to love.

III.

Knowing What We Need

Syrinx: New World Vultures

This is a poem about what is
lacking, what is absent, what is
void. It's a poem about waiting,
about wanting, about inevitability.

It's about what introverts know,
that intrinsic knowing, that
not-turning-away, that stillness,
that listening-instead, that lifting

the head, sniffing the air, that trust.
Knowing what will nourish, knowing
what we need will come. Knowing
what will be the ruin of our reputation.

Function of the Filoplume: Owl

Single-minded as all birds, eyes fixed in their sockets, Owl
is far-sighted as they come. He looks like we do: flat-faced

and dull, eyes up front for depth perception as he swoops
toward his kill in the dark. After, prey limp in his talons,

he uses the filoplume to guide to his mouth what he's unable
to see up close: the blur of what it was he was hungry for.

The Bastard Wing: Hovering Kestrel
(When Who We Are and Where We Come from Collide)

after Richard Jeffries

We are not afraid to face the wind. And if there be no wind,
we shall beat the air and dance that delicate balance: hover,

and slip, recover. Hover, and slip, recover. Wings outstretched
where mice abound, tail depressed, we heed the call of our clade

though stake our claim to what we are: birds of prey. Even
in perfect calm, gossamer falling as if these skies were raining

silk, we dance. Only the bastard wing to blame for this, all this
fateful hovering, hanging between hunger and our remorse.

Cry of the Early Moulter: Hen

All we know is that we are cold and you
are mindful of the stock pot. Cruel, cruel

fate! We itch for transformation, losing
the dead we don't need, prickly with these

pin feathers blossoming below. What is
an egg but an idea? And, oh, the careful

hatching, yellow sun too bright. Cruel fate,
that we are gone too soon, and at your hand!

That you can't see the beauty of the balding,
the sumptuous nature of moving slowly,

the richness of rest. The rested yolk is
orange fire. It warms, it nurtures, it provides.

It's the long answer to this short suffering,
less what we need than what you deserve.

Justice

Two herons were building a nest. The first one
stretched his slender neck toward the second,

who delivered the long, slim broken branches
that would fashion their home. I've always said it:

even so beautiful, birds can be cruel. The sticks
he brought her, he stole. The calls that filled the air

came from herons whose homes were being
destroyed. I'll say it again: birds rival even us

for what they do. Loving this world so much
they steal for their own survival. Keening grief

to the wind they think will hear. Believing that
someone somewhere will understand, will answer.

Brood Parasite: Screaming Cowbird

She is dull, this brown-grey bird, but no fool. She bides her time,
watching, waiting—remembering, maybe, how to mimic the call

of her own step-siblings, that hungry need: *See me here! Believe
I belong!* It goes on. Settling on the warm eggs of her shinier sister,

she lays her own and leaves. Hides. Knows she's done what's
right, for all of them. Waits again and watches, just to be sure.

What's Not in Our Nature

Still-blind honeyguide chicks,
newly hatched from their shells,
use perfectly pointed beaks
to puncture any eggs still left
in the nest. Carnivorous shrikes

impale their prey on any spike
they can find. The whole world
watched on a livestream cam
while a Pittsburgh peregrine

falcon fed one dead hatchling
to one that survived. I mean,
we'd rather not know the ways
of the wild, where our hungry
hearts might lead. We see a bird

soar and call it free, fight for
the right to live the same way,
knowing peace means nothing
to parasite, that might, on its own,

never yields to mercy. We see
ourselves as songbirds only, but
given the hunger, given the cause,
given our driving fear, we wake
up singing in the morning sun

what just doesn't jibe with the
nightly news. It helps not to turn
away from the world, to see
with grace these gifts we're given:
the will to live, this want to rise.

I Dream Myself a Bird of Prey

The hair on my legs sprouts into feathers, toes curl
into claws. My eyes focus, fierce; nose and teeth

now a horny melding. I feel my scapula, sacred,
give birth to wings. Storms come, heavy winds. I am

a lifting, a rising. I see my sisters soaring with me.
We are hungry, searching for prey, see snakes

and rats and bottom-feeding fish: we scour fields,
plunge the oceans, feast until we've had our fill.

IV.

Off Course

Thrush

One day, walking along a rural highway,
I saw a turtle up ahead in full silhouette:
the long stretch of her neck, lovely curve

of her shell. I marveled at her eagerness
to cross the road, neck so curiously long
I squinted into my approach, gradually

seeing it wasn't a turtle's neck at all, but
the tail of a fallen bird. Close enough
now to kneel carefully beside the hermit

thrush barely bigger than the palm of my
hand, I studied him closely to believe he
really was dead. One leg stretched absurdly

straight and long, foot and toes perfectly
en pointe. I couldn't see his other leg till I
turned him over, saw it curled up tightly

against his body on the other side. Each eye
a small black crater, I guessed he'd been
there a pretty good while. I wanted to be

on my way, but meeting the thrush had
thrown me off my game. I wanted to be
done with telling this story, any story,

wanted Earth and Sky to tell me they had
no more gifts to give, and here was this
turtle become bird before me, symbol

of earth turned to spirit of death. I turned
to the wind and howled. *Have at me!* I cried.
What else ya got? I can take it! I opened my

arms to all of it and heard the rumble of
a car, heard it before it appeared: older
model, beat up, nondescript, white sedan.

Of course it was white, Oh Mechanical Spirit
of Henry Ford! Oh Spirit of Dodge and
Chrysler! Oh Toyota! Oh Honda! Oh Kia Soul!

I considered standing my ground
in the center of the road, shaking my fist
at the car. But truly—or, at least, after only

a moment's hesitation—I took no offense
at the driver's intrusion. This is how
the world works. We impose ourselves

on each other, in all kinds of ways. I let the car
pass, bowed my head as it whipped by. Clearly
the car had little interest in me or in this bird.

We live, we die, we rise again! I shouted to
the blue air all around me. But then I stopped,
cocked my ear, and listened. *Yes,* I nodded.

Yes. It's true: sometimes we just disappear.
It's important, I think, or helpful at least, to
see all the world, everything that happens

to us, as metaphor, while acknowledging
at the same time it simply is what it is.
I found a bird dead in the road. Time ebbs

and it flows. The world is a terrible, beautiful
place where those not with us are with us
all the time. All of us not dead are dying.
All of us are spirits waiting to be found.

Testament: Old, New

When the waters began to recede, Noah released both
Raven and Dove; which one returned and how many times
depends on what you read. Raven, released, may have
refused to return. Forty days trapped in a cage, flight
seems a rational response. Who returns to their captor?
Consider this raven, whom the Lord has fed, who suffers
as symbol of darkness and light. Liberated, what's left
for him on a ship that wants only a harbor? It's hollow
bone that allows each bird its flight. Consider the raven
rising, rising. Consider: why did the dove return?

Hoatzin: What We Believe

We take in too much. It's both our nature and our need:
we crave. And in our devouring, there's a secret place,
a sieve. Raptors cough up the bones. Sparrows spit out
the husk. We ruminate, you and I, a holy thing. We muse.
And when we're through? The stink of what we leave
behind, fetid? It's what sets us apart. What keeps us close.

Off Course

This morning, a hooded oriole arrived
in Ohio and settled into a blossoming
cherry tree. Strange and beautiful, this

clashing: orange bird, black mask, wild
explosion of pink all around him. He, too,
is in seclusion. They're called vagrants,

these birds blown so far off course. They
rarely survive. Not long ago, a masked
booby rode a gulf-coast hurricane north,

landed in Cape Cod and died a few days
later. It's the young adults, so unused to
traveling at all, who tend to stray like this.

(Didn't we all, once? Didn't we hope to?)
But not all the accidentals die. Darwin's
finches bloomed like these pink blossoms.

Hawaiian honeycreepers sing all across
that strand of jeweled islands. We survive
all the ways that we can, spirits blown

off course. And when we don't, we ride
currents of air that caress us all, winds
whispering: *Don't you worry, loves. Don't*

you worry. We've all been blown off course;
it doesn't mean we're lost. Hear them now,
whispering? Spirits saying, *We're still here.*

Great Lakes Waterfowl: *Rete Mirabile*

It's a heat transfer system, the wonderful net
that keeps their legs and feet from freezing:

warm blood, beating away from the heart
passes the cold blood fleeing their feet—

and those feet, just skin on bone, ingenious
design, paddle happily away, nonplussed,

gently churning the lake's silver surface,
keeping it open, keeping their deep-dive

fishy food supply available all winter long.
Birds have no fear of ice or snow or polar

vortices, no instinct for what to do when
a flash freeze screams across the lake, locking

them perfectly into place, those marvelous,
miraculous feet of so little use to them now.

Extinction: Elephant Bird

after Walton Ford's Madagascar

If Bird be spirit, Elephant speaks of love.
She might have been a god.

We hunt them down, our gods,
harness them, call them a chariot to Grace.
We ride our gods to extinction.

Elephant, ten feet tall and flightless,
laid an egg so large it could feed a family.
And so we feasted.

If Bird be spirit, and spirit something we seek,
if prayer comes close to a question,

might forgiveness be what we ask for?
Might the empty hole of our hearts
seal itself,

willing, once more, to bear the beating?

Iterative Evolution: Aldabra Rail

I.

From the headline *and don't we all know*
we can't trust headlines it seemed a bit
like Phoenix who suffered that fiery death
over and over again each time rising
from its own ashes *and don't we all know*
what that feels like, don't we all know,
we who are willing, who are able, to rise
again and again? And the article said
the flightless rail was extinct, not a single
bird but an entire species, dead and gone,
since the atoll they lived on sank below
sea level 136,000 years ago. Then it
re-evolved back into existence when
the atoll rose again, *and don't we all know*
what that feels like, don't we all know
the work that it takes, the hell that it takes,
to come back? And as beautiful and hopeful
as it seemed when I read it, the cynic in me
suspected this is too perfect a myth for
our times, this is exactly the story we
who are hopeless all need to hear: It ain't
over till it's over, by god. Glaciers are
melting and sea levels rising; okay, we
admit it, we're fucked; okay, we admit it,
we're doomed. But it won't be the end
because, now we know this oh-suddenly-
convenient evolution, we can re-evolve.
Doesn't it sound lovely, to re-evolve?
Doesn't it sound hopeful to "reclaim your
island," and doesn't it sound wonderful to "return
again and again"? Oh rare phenomenon, oh
extinction that is not the end, oh hail Mary
pass, we'll be back to inhabit this earth
forever and ever, amen.

II.

But I started with anger I didn't actually
feel until later. *An Extinct Bird Species,*
the headline said, *Has Evolved Back Into
Existence, Study Says.* Study says, so
it must be science, and isn't it poetry,
too, to evolve back into existence, and
haven't I done exactly that again and again—
and I don't just mean all the pills
that I swallowed, all the times that I died—
I mean since I started to believe in my own
holy mysticism, since I started to understand
that rollercoaster existence is not about
falling into perilous despair, it's about
the rising. I started to understand that
when those issues rose again and again—
*I am not worthy, I am not meant to be here,
I should never have been born*—I was able
to deal with them at higher and higher
levels of consciousness. My psyche was
saying, *okay, we dealt with this. Now it's
time to look again more closely. It's safe
to look again more closely.* And I've come
to understand that consciousness is kind.
I've come to understand the evolution
of a healthy mind: we rise and rise again,
each time able to fly higher and higher—
we do indeed reclaim our islands. And,
hey, isn't it lovely to know the Aldabra
rail evolved to be flightless because it had
no enemy, because it had no predator,
because it had nothing that wanted to kill it,
because it had nothing it needed to rise above?
Oh beautiful, beautiful, bird, oh bird who
knows nirvana, oh bird who has reached
perfection, oh bird who has grounded itself,
oh bird who says *let the sea rise, it is only
water, let the sea rise, we'll rise too, let
the sea rise, we are one with the sea, we are
one with all beings who shall live on this earth
forever and ever, amen.*

III.

And perhaps that's the point of perishing:
dying to know we can live, rising to know
it's best to stay grounded. But that's jumping
ahead again now, that's telling this story
in medias res. If I'm telling it right, I'm telling
you this: the Aldabra rail's resurrection
stayed with me for three full days before
I started to question the perfect poetry
of that article's headline. *Iterative Evolution:*
Did the Aldabra Rail Evolve Twice? asked
the next headline I read online, *and of course*
I found the articles online because
don't we all know we never reach further
than our phones, and I knew that the question
was rhetorical, I knew that the answer
would turn out to be no, I knew that when
a source calls itself *HowStuffWorks: Science,*
it has already set out to shoot you down.
So 248 miles north of Madagascar, Science says,
out in the Indian Ocean, there's a shallow
lagoon encircled by islands. Science likes to
start at the beginning. Science likes to use big
words and to explain things parenthetically
(like how many kilometers those miles
are equal to, that the Aldabra rail is called
Dryolimnas cuvieri aldabranus in Latin).
It likes to be sure that we all listen carefully,
likes to be sure that we all understand who's
in charge. Science goes on to explain that
the Aldabra rail is a chicken-sized bird,
that it happens to be flightless, that it evolved
from a still-living bird "that often takes to
the skies." It explains why some of these birds
can fly, why this particular bird cannot, and
it takes 288 words to come to the term
it wants to define: *iterative evolution.* To hear
some tell it, says Science, the Aldabra rail
went extinct and then resurrected itself
from the dead. That's not what happened,

says Science. It's not how iterative evolution
works. It takes another 217 words to tell us
that this is repetition and not resurrection.
When the seas went down and the atoll
resurfaced the original bird still flying returned
and, having no predator, evolved once again
to a second species of flightless rail whose
bones look almost identical to the first.
Science took 244 words to end with this:
"while natural selection is a powerful force,
it cannot revive an extinct species." It cannot
bring back the dead.

IV.

Look. I believe that science can save us,
and I believe that science proves nothing
at all. Which is to say I believe in nuance.
Which is to say I believe in opposing forces.
Which is to say I believe that good can be
evil and, yes, I believe that evil can be
good. I believe in yin and I believe in yang
and I believe that a circle can be unbroken.
Look. Phoenix is a bird that never existed.
But think of all it has taught us. The Aldabra
rail disappeared, and think of all we can
learn. We refuse to believe we are going
to die, but the death of the body is real.
That's useful to know. The life of the spirit
is harder to prove, and that in itself is reason
to live. It's useful to wonder. Look. The rail
who still lives, still flies. And the rail who
kept to the ground is gone. Do you think
either of them thought for a moment about
whether the other was real? Which is to say
that I think that when they were hungry,
they ate. When their food passed through
them, they shat. And I think that we do
the same. When we look to the skies,
we see birds of all kinds. When we dig
in the ground, we find bones. If we lift up

the bones, we can use them to beat out a rhythm
on drums, beat out a rhythm that will pulse
ever outward, beat out a rhythm that some
of us will dance to while some of us tremble
in fear. Look. Some of the dancing is conquering
fear and some of the fear is what keeps us
alive. Some of the fear is what keeps us alive.
Some of that fear is what keeps us alive. By god
we're here now, and if we stay in this moment,
that's the same as forever, and this is what
I'm trying to say. I am the rail both living and dead.
I've been to the sky, and I've kept to the ground.
I've been here forever and ever means always.
I'll be here forever and so will you, ever, and
the rail will keep coming forever and ever.
For ever and ever, amen.

V.

What's Holy

Turkey Vulture: Committee, Kettle, Wake

Some birds carry a great weight. It's what we ask
of them. It fills a need. Doves we want to be holy:

symbols of spirit so pure they have power to lift
us all. And what will vultures ever be but omens?

Something has gone wrong. Somebody has to pay.
The committee sits still in the fir tree's branches;

we're sure they plan our demise. Kettle boiling
overhead seems the same slow, languid stirring

of our own dread, that desperate, unnamed need
for forgiveness. When we see the wake, we turn

away, hide our eyes, damn these filthy birds to hell.
Creatures who, unlike us, have never killed a thing,

who, unlike us, clean the mess that's left behind.
Hear that hiss, that crackle of bone, that licking

this world clean? Offer alms to that dark spirit. Pray
he comes to your back yard. Pray he comes for you.

Alakshmi

Owl came before the light.
She will come again after.

Offer her lemons and chilis.
Leave them at your back door
and do not fear:

Darkness does not intrude
where it has not been forgotten.

My Head Is an Egg

my head is an egg, a god

giving birth to sparrows—

     more gods

Marrow

How do I become whole? I asked
the man in my dream. He laughed

and tossed me a bone. I caught it
in my mouth, swallowed it whole,

and became the bearded vulture.
Somebody asked Mother Meera,

Can you send me a sign? She said,
Isn't the joy in your heart enough?

Great Blue Heron

Once, peering over a bridge, I saw a heron flying below,
skimming the surface of a stream. Awkward, angular,

and full of grace. I remembered a scene from a movie,
missionary priest lashed to a log cross and sent downriver.

I recalled, perhaps wrongly, the calm of the sacrifice.
We call ourselves willing to commit but don't always

know what we're in for. Surprise waits on the shoreline
of every adventure we sail toward. Here, blue-grey *Christos,*

knobby-kneed and seemingly certain, flies down the center
of the stream while I, above, witnessing flight from this angle,

reel with my own revelation, wondering what Heron is
looking for and whether he left anything behind.

The Detail Left Out

I.

When his uncle sent the big crane-demon
to kill him, Krishna was so very young
the monster swallowed him whole. Once inside,
he burned with a light so bright it set fire
to the demon's mouth. Krishna was vomited
out unharmed, and the demon died.

II.

Every god has a story of burning: Ra and Oyá.
Agni, Fiji, Vulcan. The bright red bush who
called to Moses. Good and evil, always paired,
create the complicated story of divine energy.

III.

The crimson-crowned Indian sarus crane,
world's tallest flying bird, mates for life.
Losing that mate, it starves itself to death.
What's left when the crane is gone, grief
nothing now but hollow bone? The greater
good, perhaps. Yearning its own forging.

IV.

Indian sarus cranes mate in the rainy season,
trumpet loudly from a coiled trachea, engage
in a spectacular display of calling and posturing.
They raise their young in an island nest
completely unconcealed. What more godly
creature than this? Still: crow, dingo, kite.

V.

Such is the power of Krishna. The burning
bush was left unharmed. Is the lesson really
that only good prevails, or can we call struggle
itself a saving? Consider the crane. Study
that spectacular display. Remember that,
separated, there is only the starving.

A Lesson in Possibilities: Mud Swallow

The Christ-child, still a working man's son, sculpted birds
of clay from the damp earth, sighed softly and released them
to the mayhem of blue skies. Still they skitter and glide.

The child trusted his hands to other miracles: water and wine,
raising the dead. As if, like so many sons, he felt the need
to prove himself, over and over again, to a distant and silent

father. As the story goes, seeing the child now buried in a tomb,
God heaved a sigh of sorrow and shame. It was the final breath
of an old testament: what the boy is capable of teaching the man.

Kleptoparasitism: Brahminy Kite

Brahminy kite, a beautiful bird, is said to have
very weak feet. He carries only very small prey.

Brahminy kite is largely a scavenger, feeding
mostly on dead fish and crabs. He's also a thief.

Brahminy kite steals the prey of other birds.
steals from dolphins, steals honey from bees.

Brahminy kite, legend tells us, is born of fire,
is called Garuda, is big enough to block the sun.

Brahminy kite, legend tells us, bears Vishnu,
who dreams the world into being, on his back.

Brahminy kite, legend tells us, is only half bird.
Half human, Garuda is much like us: beautiful,

hungry, weak, willing to cheat and steal, heavy
with the burden of sleeping gods on our backs.

European Goldfinch: An Ekphrastic

after Leonardo da Vinci's Madonna Litta

Almost an afterthought, near-hidden in the shadow of a fat baby Jesus
suckling the absurdly placed teat of a smiling Madonna, this tiny bird,

bloody-headed and aware of its shame, offers us our own absurdities:
what we are willing to believe, what we are willing to ignore. Worship

of creamy white flesh. The sacred feminine, misaligned. The sacrifice
of children, heralded as proof of what we say we believe in. Oh, spirit,

icon of death and healing and resurrection, let us pray to believe in you,
which is to say, us, which is to say, destruction. And all that comes after.

Mammals: Simurgh, Whale

She is large, as large as thirty birds, large enough
to lift a whale in her claws. And she is old, 1,700

years, old enough to have seen the world destroyed
three times. She is sacred union between earth and sky,

messenger and mediator between the two. Why
would a bird carry a whale? Perhaps to sing

their sameness. I have plunged the depths of this
blue sky, says Bird. I have soared the height of this

blue sea, says Whale. These are stories they'll tell
their nursing children. See that surface, there, below?

See that surface above? Look past the mire of mirrors,
love. See our sister soaring. Watch her dive, divine.

Lessons in the Drinking of Nectar: Hummingbird

for D. C. Glebe

Desire is a guiding force.
The ecstasy of wanting
draws us all to the feast.

***

Embrace contradiction.
Wings ablur, hover still
before the blossom,
poised for penetration.
(If, diverted, you must,
dart quickly. Strike deadly.
Come back to poise.)

***

Understand yourself a god,
deserving. See the nectary
a vessel humbling itself,
needs of its own.

***

Remember your destiny.
The long, slender syringe
of your beak. The dark line
of your vessel's deep throat.

***

Release your tongue and
drink: draw back into you
that which sustains you.
Drink, oh Divine!

***

Accept this: etymology.
Nectar is from the Greek.
Nek, death. *Tar,* overcoming.
Know you are ready. Trust
that you will live forever.

Celestial Navigation: Indigo Bunting

A star by itself doesn't say anything. —Richard Emlen

First, indigo is illusion. For a bird brighter than a sapphire sky,
bunting is the color that calls to mind our catechism: we are dust,

and to dust we shall return. What do we gain, I wonder, believing
that bird is blue? And what have we gained, knowing that bird

finds his way through the dark following the same bright star
that led wise men through the desert, to a woman big with God?

It was a god who taught us that. Or, rather, a man jealous as all gods,
who wanted only to know, who took away the sky and watched

a bird he believed was blue falter, then brought the stars back
and shouted *hallelujah,* as if the wise had not known all along:

chin up, keep steady. Make no mistake: this is not a story about faith.
It's about what we ought to be able to intuit. We are made of earth

and that is beauty enough. We know where we're headed. We can
feast when we get there knowing this: the same star guides us home.

Blood Feather

Old enough, wise, Feather lets go. Young and broken, he bleeds.
What's in between is hollow channel, filling need: we breathe,

we grow, we flounder, we fly. We are fed what we need. And
when we're not, who suffers most but Sky? The greatest wound

is often the same as the greatest gift. But not always. There
are times a wound just bleeds, its own gaping. Loss on loss.

When a broken blood feather calls, hold spirit in your hands.
Don't let go. Don't even breathe till you've come to know this:

breath is bird is sky is hand is wound is love is you is me is bird.
We are all gaping, all wound. We are all channel, filling need.

We are all Feather, whole and healed. We are all wise enough
to know when to hold on, tightly, and when, at last, to let go.

The Grateful Nature of Our Despair

There's lesson in this: that the goose gains
its flight feathers only when the gosling
learns to fly. It's the energy of the empty
nest. What tears from us, what is torn.
When a house settles, its sigh, more moan
than groan, acknowledges all of what it must
bear. Despair and hope. Grace. Drudgery.
Heavy gifts, this. Humanity.

Moss, the empty lichen, the glistening fern.
All this grows from our decay. The blossoming
fungus, rose on rose, the golden glow
of our desire. Listen: what we need is not
the same as who we are, and who we are
is who we were, now changed. Change
is constant. We're our own becoming: Father
become the Holy Son. Mother become
the Motherless Child. Feel the need for nurturing.
Nurture yourself.

Part of the politics of who we are is
the grateful nature of our own despair. We evolve,
revolve, devolve, invent. We are proton,
neutron, electrolyte, trilobite. The push and pull
of what we need to get by. Mashable. Malleable.
Meek. Roadkill, road, the sky around us watching:
cheep and chirp, roar and chatter. We are
what sloughs off, what grows back, the stump,
the vein, the reaching. We are what we think
we cannot find.

What sets us apart is not the Wasteland
we once thought. Leaves falling like so many
birds—call that the cry of the early moulter!
It's simple gathering, ashes to ashes, dust
to dust. Let grief lie there. Do not despair
of despairing. The last, sticky thread of our
desire is what pulls us all together. It should.
We turn our backs, but the light always behind us
tells us what we might have learned—

and still can. It's a crippling kind of love, this
not being who we are. It's the same history
that gives us hope, the same sticky thread
that pulls us through.

Frost on morning meadow is the first sign
of freeze. Silver-grey. What we already know.
Death awaits and is not death. Life abounds
and is not life. We are not what we fear. We are
everything we see and hear and taste and touch.
Sniff that—we are what we think offends.
We've forgotten what ferment can teach us.
Rot is a ruler used to measure what comes back
to us, and here is the secret we already know:
it all comes back. Rot is kind if we are not afraid.

You know that fear repels? That resistance really
is futile? We can't run from what is sure
to follow. But we can stand still. Calm follows
the raging river rushing toward that Great Fall.
What's left but peace and quiet, the silence
which is never silent—how could it be,
when it has so much to say? The world sees itself
in crisis. And is wrong. We've only to listen
to the cracked skull and filthy bones of what was
once called augury. Where up is down, down
is up. Rising and falling are all the same. This
is my manifesto: Hear me. Listen to the light
that guides us.

We are grit and greed and gravity's
rainbow. We are rain, falling. The bald-faced
mountain. The bold-faced lie. Boulder,
shoulder, manatee, man. Might. We are need.
We shatter the husk of human coil, enter
the quiet to find that silence, never silent.
Listen! Respond! You are not imagining things.
The push and pull of all that we need
is all that we have. What can wait is more
than we're aware of. What needs change
is only our awareness. Listen to that lovely sound:

the train, the toad, the ten-year-old. The skull
beneath our skin. There's a Temple of Knowing,
and it's not within. Human nature is part
and parcel of a more divine protocol. Hair shirt
and thistle down. Tooth and nail. What
the inside pushes out, what has function
and no need for name. Maelstrom. Madness.
Mayhem. The inner ear, worth hearing.

Sky Burial: Generosity

Scent of juniper lingering still,
the bone breakers laugh
as holy eagles feast on the flesh.

Then, bones pulverized,
mixed with tsampa, the crows
and hawks are also fed.

Satiated, the dakinis lift the soul
to the waiting wind,
ready now for what comes next.

Acknowledgments

Sincere thanks to the following journals, anthologies, presses, and organizations who have supported this work and/or published a number of these poems, some in slightly different form:

Aesthetica Magazine Creative Writing Annual: "Lessons in the Drinking of Nectar: Hummingbird"
The Blue Max Review: "Huff Post Science News Headline, or When You Wish Something More Had Been Lost"
Heartwood: "What They Imply by Depicting a Vulture" (Heartwood Broadside Winner, 2019)

"Anatomy of Birds, Part 1: Furcula" appeared in *Malala: Poems for Malala Yousafzai* (FutureCycle Press, 2013).

"Anatomy of Birds, Part 2: Common Loon," "Blood Feather," "Brood Parasite: Screaming Cowbird," "Evolution of the Eyelid: The Business of Seeing," "Function of the Filoplume: Owl," "Great Blue Heron," "Losing the Egg Tooth," "The Bastard Wing: Hovering Kestrel," "The Chicken, the Egg," "The Cry of the Early Molter," "The Grateful Nature of Our Despair," "The Insistent Nature of Acknowledging Need: Male Swan," "The Non-Euclidean Geometry of Human Existence," The Transformative Nature of Disguise: Penguin," and "Ubiquity: Sparrow" appeared in the chapbook *The Ecstasy of Wanting* (Full/Crescent, 2018).

"Alakshmi," "A Lesson in Possibilities: Mud Swallow," "Celestial Navigation: Indigo Bunting," "Chick Ornamentation: American Coot," "European Goldfinch: an Ekphrastic," "Hoatzin: What We Leave Behind," "How History Helps Us Survive: Hoatzin," "Kleptoparasitism: Brahminy Kite," "Mammals: Simurgh, Whale," "Marrow," "my head is an egg, a god," "Syrinx: New World Vultures," "Sky Burial: Generosity" and "Turkey Vulture: Committee, Kettle, Wake" appeared in *A Lesson in Possibilities* (self-published with support from Greater Columbus Arts Council, 2019).

"Gape: Fledglings" appeared in the Portfolio of the Fall 2013 Letterpress Printing & Fine Press Publishing Seminar for Emerging Writers. (The New York Center for Book Arts, 2013).

"Justice" first appeared in *Eclipsing the Dark: The Sun & Moon Poetry Festival 2014-2019* (OPA, 2020).

"Off Course" appeared in *Hyacinth* (self-published, 2020).

"Testament: Old, New," "The Detail Left Out," "Thrush," and "Routine," appeared in *How to See the World* (Bottom Dog, 2020).

Gratitude to the poetry community of Columbus, Ohio, for listening to these poems during the development of this manuscript, for their encouragement and enthusiasm, for the shining example of their own work and voices. I'm grateful, too, for the wider network of voices across Ohio and the organizations that work so hard to bring them together.

Special thanks to Susan Hendrickson, Richard Carr, and George Looney.

Eternal thanks and love to Michael Perkins.

About FutureCycle Press

FutureCycle Press is dedicated to publishing lasting English-language poetry in both print-on-demand and Kindle formats. Founded in 2007 by long-time independent editor/publishers and partners Diane Kistner and Robert S. King, the press was incorporated as a nonprofit in 2012. A number of our editors are distinguished poets and writers in their own right, and we have been actively involved in the small press movement going back to the early seventies.

Each year, we award the FutureCycle Poetry Book Prize and honorarium for the best original full-length volume of poetry we published that year. Introduced in 2013, proceeds from our Good Works projects are donated to charity. Our Selected Poems series highlights contemporary poets with a substantial body of work to their credit; with this series we strive to resurrect work that has had limited distribution and is now out of print.

We are dedicated to giving all of the authors we publish the care their work deserves, offering a catalog of the most diverse and distinguished work possible, and paying forward any earnings to fund more great books. All of our books are kept "alive" and available unless and until an author requests a title be taken out of print.

We've learned a few things about independent publishing over the years. We've also evolved a unique and resilient publishing model that allows us to focus mainly on vetting and preserving for posterity poetry collections of exceptional quality without becoming overwhelmed with bookkeeping and mailing, fundraising activities, or taxing editorial and production "bubbles." To find out more about what we are doing, come see us at futurecycle.org.

The FutureCycle Poetry Book Prize

All original, full-length poetry books published by FutureCycle Press in a given calendar year are considered for the annual FutureCycle Poetry Book Prize. This allows us to consider each submission on its own merits, outside of the context of a traditional contest. Too, the judges see the finished book, which will have benefitted from the beautiful book design and strong editorial gloss we are famous for.

The book ranked the best in judging is announced as the prize-winner in January of the subsequent year. There is no fixed monetary award; instead, the winning poet receives an honorarium of 20% of the total net royalties from all poetry books and chapbooks the press sold online in the year the winning book was published. The winner is also accorded the honor of being on the panel of judges for the next year's competition; all judges receive copies of the contending books to keep for their personal library.

www.ingramcontent.com/pod-product-compliance
Lightning Source LLC
Chambersburg PA
CBHW070042110426
42741CB00036B/3162